Successful Entrepreneurship

A practical guide

By Dr. Carl Marx

Copyright © 2018 by Dr. Carl Marx

All rights reserved. This book or any portion thereof may not be reproduced or used in any manner whatsoever without the express written permission of the publisher except for the use of brief quotations in a book review.

For Lenél

Table of Content

Introduction	3
Focus, Focus and Focus	6
The Job of the Entrepreneur	10
Focus Areas	10
Main Activities	15
Planning	15
Organizing	15
Leading	16
Controlling	17
Play to Your Strengths	18
Cash is King	24
Budgeting	29
The Monthly Cash Budget	30
The Daily Cash Budget	30
Managing Funds at Hand	31
Keeping Cash on Hand	33
Understanding Profit and Loss	34
The Profit and Loss Statement	35
The P&L Statement Frequency	36
The P&L Statement Structure	37
Calculating Profit and Loss	38
Uses of the Profit and Loss Account	40

Why is the Paperwork Necessary	41
I Got Too Much Debt, What Now?	**42**
Getting Out of Your Debt Spiral	42
The Road to Recovery	43
Evaluate the Path to Your Current Financial Position	43
Objectively Assess Your Financial Situation	44
Negotiate With Creditors	45
Avoid New Debts	46
Control Spending	47
Increase Income	48
Final Words	49
Using Financial Statements for Decision-making	**50**
The Financial Statements	50
Purpose of Financial Statements	51
Measurement & Evaluation	52
Interpreting the Numbers	52
The Time Value of Money	**54**
Comparing Different Times	55
Present Value	56
Future Value	57
Discounting	58
Market and Sell	**60**

Marketing	**61**
Marketing Research	62
Strategic Marketing	63
Operational Marketing	65
Selecting the Optimum Marketing Mix	**66**
Using & Understanding the 4 P's Marketing Mix Model	67
Product Decisions	68
Price Decisions	69
Promotion Decisions	69
Place Decisions	70
Marketing Tools	**71**
Brochures	72
Mailers	73
Posters	74
Business Cards	75
Loyalty Cards	75
Electronic Marketing	76
Sales	**78**
Run a Professional Business	**80**
Conclusion	**84**
References	**85**

Successful Entrepreneurship

A practical guide

Why this book?

Once my son wanted to enter the family business I got him to start on his own first to allow him to do what he wanted without my interference. I soon realized that he was very willing to work very hard but that he will not achieve the success that he could without additional knowledge about business. After we had a number of discussions, I realized that what I may take for granted and general knowledge, due to my years of experience and academic background, is valuable to startup entrepreneurs. I then started writing down some of my thoughts to give my son some form of reference. This was the beginning of this book

How to use this book:

This book is not a step-by-step guide to success for the startup entrepreneur. It contains a combination of content I feel the startup entrepreneur should not miss when setting up a venture. I strongly recommend that the book is read in its entirety, and the concepts evaluated based on the site-specific micro and macro socio-economic factors prevailing.

In the book, I am not trying to provide you with a checklist of items that you should do to make you successful. Success is never that simple. You should read the book for understanding and implement concepts that apply to your situation rather than blindly follow the examples.

Legal Disclaimer

The information provided in this book is of a general nature only. It does NOT take into account your objectives, financial situation and needs. Before acting on any information contained in this book you should consider the appropriateness of the advice having regard to your objectives, financial situation and needs. The book should not be your only source of business information. Each financial situation is different. The information provided is.

It is recommended that you seek professional guidance form you financial or legal advisors for information specific to your situation as appropriate.

All of the best with your business venture

Dr. Carl Marx

Page intentionally left blank

Introduction

One of the primary problems that face first-time entrepreneurs is that they often face a perfect storm. They often lack governance and financial skills, face a shortage of investors prepared to finance their business, have to overcome a regulatory environment that was developed for big businesses. In short, start-up

Entrepreneurs are often technical experts (in some field that they have worked in before) and do not have the skills and knowledge in the areas required to effectively capitalize on a business opportunity.

The next problem most start-up entrepreneurs face it to select the correct business idea to convert into a business. It is a fact that business ideas abound, and to top it, there are no real bad business ideas, in fact it is mostly the matching of the idea with the skill set of the first-time entrepreneur and the execution of the idea that makes some observers think that some ideas are bad and others are better.

There is no magic wand, or secret formula, that will ensure success in business. In order to improve the chances for business success for start-up entrepreneurs, I have assembled a number of top tips in this e-book from various sources that should be useful for most first-time entrepreneurs when embarking upon their business journey.

Studying, adapting it to your situation and then utilizing the tips in this e-book will not ensure success but I am convinced that it will it will improve your chances of success significantly.

It is said that the core principles Steve Jobs instilled in Apple is the need to stay focused on doing only what you do best. It is easy to add more lines but it is hard to stay focused on what counts.

Focus, Focus and Focus

As a startup Entrepreneur, one of the hardest decisions you will have to make is what not to work on.

There are literally millions of sources for business ideas and this is not necessarily a good thing. One of the biggest mistakes new start-up entrepreneurs make is to leap at too many "opportunities" they stumble upon without considering the fit of the opportunity to their current situation. Issues that should be considered include available skills, experience and funds, to name but a few.

When I tell entrepreneurs to focus they think I mean that they have to say yes to only the thing that fits into their business model. The truth of the matter is that focus means to say no to all those many opportunities that come along to divert your attention from your selected opportunity, whether they fit in or not. A good thing to remember is to focus on quality, not quantity. Make use of some of the information contained in this e-book and select one, yes I am really saying one business idea and pursue it until successful. You need to remember that all business opportunities are not, necessarily suited to all entrepreneurs.

It is extremely important to focus in order to improve your chances for success. Not spreading yourself too thin by getting involved in too many business ideas at the same time is one of the critical components for success. If you focus on a single opportunity at a time, it will ensure that you can be more efficient and effective. Having less diverse problems to solve will result in your productivity increasing dramatically. In addition, you will be dealing with less diverse activities by dealing with one business idea at a time, you will be focused and as a result, make fewer mistakes.

The problem with having to deal with multiple business ideas at the same time is that time becomes your enemy and you, therefore, tend to rush decisions that normally leads to more mistakes. The question, however, is what business idea to focus on. In order to ensure that your focus is maintained by the selected business idea, it is important to select an idea that you have some experience in. It should also be something that you like, as you will probably spend the next few years taking this business idea from a concept to a fully-fledged business. If you select a business opportunity purely because you feel that it may make lots of money for you, you already are at a disadvantage. The real challenge does is not in starting a business venture, the challenge is to grow from a startup subsistence entrepreneur to a sustainable business. This takes persistence and lots of focus.

The vast majority of successful entrepreneurs start with one business at a time. Sometimes they have to start over because it takes a few tries to get it right. However, they very seldom run more than one business venture at the same time, they sequence it and transfer the lessons learnt from the one to the next.

There is no truth or logic to the idea that more is better when it comes to entrepreneurs and businesses, the answer lies in focus.

In order to keep focus, it is important to have a clear vision for where you want your business to go and by when. Keep in mind that challenges will arise along the way, and therefore, if you are not 100% sure where you are heading, the different opportunities that present themselves itself along the way will draw your attention away from your main vision.

One of the most successful entrepreneurs I have met wrote down his vision and pasted copies on his morning mirror, to remind him where he wants to go.

Entrepreneurs must keep their focus on their

companies and the goals they set for themselves. Greatness in business is not achieved by trying something new every time one of your friends or acquaintances tells you about the latest thing that makes money. This is achieved by avoiding situations that could distract you from your business goals. It may not be possible to avoid every single detracting situation, but it is well worth the effort to evaluate situations with this in mind. In order to ensure that your activities are focused securely on those issues that will allow you to achieve your goals, it is important to know what the business drivers and other important components of your business are.

The Job of the Entrepreneur

Focus Areas

Over the years, I have discovered that some issues that look important may not always be that important. A number of entrepreneurs that I have consulted for to try to prevent than from losing everything they worked for have one thing in common. They were the entrepreneur but acted like employees. This is not strange as when starting up a new small business the entrepreneur often works like an employee and more often than not is the company. What often goes wrong is that some of the entrepreneurs do not grow out of the initial operational position, to take on the bigger roles as needed. This, more often than not, leads to a catastrophic failure of the venture.

I believe that you should focus on the following seven issues to make a success of your business. In some types of industries, the priorities may be different from in others, but as far as I am concerned, these are always important.

Successful entrepreneurs are those individuals

who know what needs to be done when and then focus on that. You need to understand the difference between important and urgent clearly. I have heard someone said one day that it is important to call back the bank manager if you receive a message to do so, but it is urgent to shut down a machine when unexpected smoke rises from it. With determining priorities comes the need to manage your time and avoid preventable and distracting situations

A successful entrepreneur will always know more about the flow of money in and out of the business than about the production or other issues in the companies. The entrepreneur does not have to be an accountant but needs to have a detailed understanding of the finances of the business. This includes:

- The total revenue as well as that of each business section,
- The margins and how they compare to that of the competitors,
- The operational expenses and how close these are to budgeted numbers,
- Progress on capital expenses,
- The profit, and how this compares to budget.

The entrepreneur should daily know how much money is in each bank account and how much will be needed the next day to pay bills. In most countries, it is a criminal offence not to pay salaries and wages on time.

Customers are the lifeblood of any business; in fact, I have often heard a particularly successful entrepreneur tell his employees that the person that just left the shop is the one who pays all their salaries. Remember that everything that brings in money into the company is bought by somebody, that is called customers. Entrepreneurs should only spend personal time with customers and potential customers, but also ensure that every employee understands the importance of treating customers correctly.

Coming up with suitable solutions to the problems your company is facing or will be facing in the future is also a primary task of the entrepreneur. In this case, I do not imply that you should solve the production problems of, say a burnt out motor on the plant, or obtaining a credit note from a supplier when something was sent back. If you have people you pay to do these things, you need to allow them to get on with their work and do what you pay them to do. You should be looking at your sales forecast and compare that with the sales budget, and if there is a significant difference or a negative trend it is your job to get the relevant person or teams to come up with potential solutions that you may approve reject or recommend adjustments. If there is, for example, a continued trend that certain motors in the production plant keep on burning out, you need to let your maintenance and production teams come up with a solution that you should evaluate.

As the business grows you will need to appoint a suitable and a sufficient number of people to assist in doing some of the tasks in the business. It is extremely important to know some of the basic labour law requirements for your own country and industry before you jump into this. I know of a number of small businesses that have outsourced their human resources function completely. They pay a company a basic fee as a retainer for a certain number of predefined tasks. These may include onboarding of new employees, hearing disciplinary cases and keeping labour contracts up to legal specifications. It is up to you to decide what you feel comfortable handling in-house and what to include in an outsourcing contract. As an entrepreneur, you should spend a part of our day call on your individual workers on the shop floor to establish if they are busy with work activities and suitably trained to do their jobs effectively.

One of the overarching jobs of any entrepreneur is coaching his employees. You need to get into the habit of asking questions rather than giving solutions. Gone are the days that you are in charge because you know more than the next person does. The key to staying ahead of the curve in so far as your employees are concerned is not to try and know more than they do, but to know enough to ask the correct questions. It is also important to, more often than not, ask a question for which you already know the answer. This sounds counter-intuitive, but the value of this lies in it that you can ask the questions in such a manner that the individual will discover the answer for him or herself. The advantage of this is that that individual will own the solution and will, therefore, make sure it is implemented successfully. I have often seen how a very good solution to a problem fails because the boss tells the subordinate what to do to solve the problem.

Main Activities

To make a comprehensive list of all the main activities are almost impossible. What I will try to provide here is a summary of some of those activities that you cannot go ignored. I will use the basic framework provided by Louis A. Allen starting in 1958 through a number of publications up until 1996.

Planning

Everybody knows that planning is important. The saying, if you don't know where you're going, any road will take you there from Alice in Wonderland is probably the most quoted when trying to explain the importance of planning. If you do no other planning but ensure your business plan is complete and comprehensive it will allow you to get a long way. There are a number of books on this subject, which you may wish to consult if needed.

Organizing

In respect of organizing one of the more important issues to remember as an entrepreneur is to make sure you delegate effectively. Too often the startup entrepreneur wants to do everything himself as he thinks that he can do the job better than anybody else, or that there is not enough time to explain the task to somebody else and then to still correct the mistakes afterwards.

The truth of the matter is that this is not a sustainable model and is even less scalable. If you cannot delegate effectively you will, at best always be a startup, but probably fail as an entrepreneur.

Leading

Leading is probably your main function but what does is the practical implications of that. My view of leadership is that you have to consult but be firm in making decisions that affect the business. You have to do everything needed to ensure that your team(s) stay motivated. (This does not include paying them more than you should). One of the dimensions of leadership that a lot of entrepreneurs (and even executives of large companies) neglect, is to develop their team members through personal coaching.

Controlling

Your second most important task is to make sure that things actually happen as planned. Some call it controlling others call it a follow-up. Whatever you call it, there is no option for you not to put time aside and focus on this important task. The best way to do it is to make sure everybody understand what will be viewed as the measure of beings successful. The next step is to measure performance regularly and objectively. Once you have the performance results compare them to the standard you set and establish deviations. Finally, develop plans to correct any deviations.

Play to Your Strengths

This may sound like an obvious statement you may say, as "who will attempt a business idea that he or she does not know anything about", you may ask. In reality, many business ideas fail because of this exact cause. Often, new entrepreneurs are duped into a business opportunity because of the promise of huge financial returns. The reality often is that some special skill or knowledge is required to secure the returns that the entrepreneur does not have.

To this end, it is important that an entrepreneur needs to know and recognize his or her strengths and abilities. Just as important is to do a proper introspection and expose the blind spots where the lack of skills and abilities often lay hidden. In other words, you do not know what you do not know and you, therefore, have to work hard to try to find out what you do not know. More often than not, you will regret thinking you knew all the answers instead of spending time listening to others who wanted to give you advise.

Once you have identified your own strengths and weaknesses more informed decisions can be made about business opportunities that are identified. Any business opportunity that you want to capitalize on that requires you to make use of your strengths and abilities will have a significantly larger chance of succeeding than the other way around, irrespective of the so-called potential of the opportunity.

In order for any start-up entrepreneur to successfully execute any business idea, there are three primary questions you have to ask yourself about the idea.

Question 1: Do I have the skills knowledge and experience to make this business idea successful.

It is true that you could hire some specialists to do the work on your behalf, but this comes with its own challenges, and should not be the first solution. You should have an intimate working knowledge of at least the technical aspects of the execution of the tasks associated with the business idea. It is not only good from a cost perspective for a startup business if the entrepreneur does the work that is expected from workers that will be appointed later, it also allows you to coach, evaluated and assist future employees to work the way you would like them to. In truth, a large number of successful entrepreneurs are people that turned their hobbies into a business.

Question 2: Will the business be able to generate

sufficient funds to pay for itself.

The truth of the matter is that No one will give you money. Yes, you heard correctly, no one (not even banks) would give you money to start a business if you cannot prove to them that they will get their money back. The best way to prove this is to prove that the business will generate sufficient cash flow to pay back the loan and interest as and when such payments become payable. If you need a large investment to start your business idea that you cannot get, you have different options to consider.

You can go back to the drawing board, redefine your starting point, and grow your business to a point where it has proven itself. This can be achieved by scaling down start-up plans that may be outside your own capability to finance. Another approach could be to simplify the idea until it is manageable as an early stage business and keep the big expense items for later in the growth of the business when free cash is more available to service loans. Another is to find ways to prove your business model using your selected business idea on a minimalistic budget and generate free cash that way. One way of doing this is accessing government funds for start-up businesses or setting up your business in an incubator-site for start-up businesses.

Question 3: Do I have sufficient assets to attract investments that will not dilute my shareholding in my business venture to a point where I lose control.

Even banks will ask this question when you approach them but remember the first two questions are more important to them as they do not want to own your assets, they want you to pay them back the loan amount with interest as that is their business. You should also be wary that not all assets should be put at risk, even if you are "100% sure" of success. Items like the house you live in should be an asset of last resort. In other words, protect certain of your assets and do not sign this over as surety to anyone in exchange for money that you want to invest in your new business venture.

Investors who may be more interested in the answer to this question are normally investors who would like to invest in your business as a shareholder. The downside to this is that you give away a portion of your business and the associated control. There are no real hard and fast rules about shareholder investors. It is important to make determine how important control over your business is for you. If you wish to keep control over your business, you should be very careful when considering this option as even minor shareholders can have a significant impact on how a business is run.

Another aspect to consider is that the later in the lifetime of your business venture, you seek shareholder investors, the more expensive the shares will be and therefore the more cash injection your business will receive. It is always better to demonstrate your worth before looking for a shareholder investment unless you have no other choice. Once your business venture is proven to be successful (even on a small scale), your chances of raising capital from investors will improve dramatically.

They key here is to grow your business to prove your concept, market and capacity to generate revenue from a startup to a sustainable business venture before you approach shareholder investors.

Page intentionally left blank

Cash is King

It is very, very important for any start-up entrepreneur to always make sure that the cash needs of the business are well understood and that there is and will be enough cash in the bank to deal with the cash flow needs of the business. It is a well-known fact that the most common business-failure mode by far is running out of cash.

Cash is the oil that lubricates the wheels of your economic success. Without oil machines normally seizes up and comes to a grinding halt. Without sufficient cash, you will not be able to do anything, much like a machine without oil.

On the other hand, keeping cash can be a very expensive exercise, since cash is a non-income earning asset. The aim of money management is to minimize the amount that you need to keep in order to service your normal amount needed without losing out on special discounts, ensuring that you will maintain an acceptable credit rating and to meet unexpected needs for immediate money.

Businesses run out of cash for a wide variety of reasons. Two of the more important reasons why startup businesses run out of cash are discussed below. There may be exceptions to these for a few types of start-up businesses but the reality is these principles are mostly universal.

The first drain on cash is that owners often do not act like the owner of a startup. They often focus on having fancy offices, expensive cars and big entertainment accounts. All these can be big, and often unnecessary, drain on cash.

The next squeeze on cash may be less obvious to some. This is when a business is allowed grow too fast. The start-up entrepreneur often falls into the trap to allow their companies to grow too fast. During a growing phase, the pressure on cash is increased as most companies experience an increase in debtors that need to be financed with own funds.

Your wallet is your business' life-blood. Practice and perfect the art of being frugal. Watch every dollar and triple-check every expense. Maintain a low overhead and manage your cash flow effectively.

One of the first things any start-up entrepreneur should learn is to focus on your finances. Make sure that you know this dimension of your business inside out. If you don't know your revenues, expenses, capital requirements, profits (gross and net), debt, cash flow, and effective tax rate (among other things) you are asking for trouble. Big trouble.

It is a fact that one of the biggest challenges that startup businesses face is a lack of proper financial management. In one study, it was found that eighty percent of small businesses did not keep proper financial books or financial accounting system. The basic steps:

1. Smart cash flow management starts with financial projections. They are an early warning system that helps you anticipate cash flow peaks and valleys for the coming year.
2. Make cash flow projections for the business and compare them to actual results during the year. It is common even for large and profitable companies to go out of business because they ran out of cash. This can be prevented with suitable and sufficient cash flow management.
3. Make it a habit to monitor cash inflows and outflows. This will result in you having a feeling for the cash position of your business and result in you having an "early warning" when cash will be tight.

4. A careful analysis of the reasons for your cash balance (high or low) is vital to making the correct business decisions that will not end up in the business running out of cash.
5. Monitoring your cash flow as the year progresses is one of the most important things you can do to track the financial pulse of your business. How to boost cash flow:
    a. Plan Expenditure. Determine your financing needs when making your financial projections. When you approach your bank well ahead of time they are normally more willing to provide cash flow bridging than when you are in trouble already. Having well-prepared cash flow projections gives your banker the confidence that you know what is going on in your business as one would expect from a good manager.
    b. Evaluate financing terms when considering financing to alleviate cash flow pressures, be sure to assess the interest rate (fixed or floating), the size of the financing, security requirements the bank

needs and the amortization period. Only by evaluating all of these factors and conducting a parallel evaluation of your cash flow forecast can a suitable decision be made.

c. Utilize supplier financing Many startup businesses do not make use of this valuable source of financing as they either do not know about the option or think that it is only for larger businesses. The format of supplier financing can take various forms. From a standard 30-, 60- or 90-day payment plan to a full consignment stock option for trade stock. For capital items, suppliers often have a more beneficial financing option than banks.

d. Continuously assess the cost of financing as macroeconomic conditions change so does the cost of finance. In cases where a fixed interest rate was accepted and general interest rates decline it could be useful to retire or reduce that loan amount.

Other options are to evaluate the impact of refinancing on cash flow as an option to free up some cash flow. The tool mostly used to achieve this is the cash budget. In this section, we will investigate this budget tool.

Budgeting

You should determine your need for hard currency as part of your personal budgeting process. The budgeting process includes forecasting for acquiring both long and short-term assets.

Combining the forecasting information about expenses with expected income cash flows is called the cash budget. This budget reveals your expected cash in- and outflows over a given period.

It is a good practice to have this budget drafted at monthly intervals for a period looking forward to a year. In addition to this, a more detailed daily (or at worst weekly) the budget must also be generated for the coming month. The monthly budget is used for planning purposes and the daily budget for actual cash control.

The Monthly Cash Budget

The monthly budget is the forecast of the expected cash in and outflows for every month of the annual forecast. It reflects these figures as accurately as possible to provide you with a tool to plan when any particular purchase should be made using the funds in your current account.

It is important to note that in this type of budget only cash items are reflected. Items such as depreciation should not be included as it does not influence the flow of funds at hand. Every single expected cash item should be included in the budget. For information on step by step instructions on how to compile a cash budget please read my ezine article on this topic.

The Daily Cash Budget

The daily cash budget is a reflection of the actual money flows and provides the ideal tool to control your actual available funds on a daily basis. By updating the balance on a daily basis and updating the budget prior to making any payment you can determine if you will stay within your cash balance target. You will also be able to plan for making more funds available by calling up short-term investments to be available to make these payments.

Managing Funds at Hand

It is true that money in your till does not generate any income and therefore the ideal is to have as little cash at hand as possible while still being in a position to take care of your responsibilities. You should remember that you could make various income generating instruments instead of keeping it readily available. There are basically three motives why people will keep some cash at hand.

The first and most obvious motive to keep money at hand is to be able to continue to do transactions. You may reason that you could do this on credit, however, you need to establish what is financially more beneficial, to buy on credit and have no or little negotiating ability or to buy with cash and negotiate discounts and be in a better bargaining position for delivery and other extras. The amount of money you need to keep available to satisfy this motive will depend on your lifestyle, the quantity and size of regular purchases done as well as the type of purchases you intend to make.

The second motivation not to invest all your money in long-term instruments is the precautionary motive. Most households will need some cash to prepare for some unforeseen event. The magnitude of this amount will of cause vary depending on the risk appetite, the security of income inflows (such as salaries and wages) and the value of available funds set aside for this purpose.

The third motivation for keeping currency on hand is to take advantage of potential situations that may occur that would require one to have money to take advantage of opportunities. As it is mostly an issue that you cannot plan for in detail an objective assessment of this is not possible and each individual will consider what the magnitude of the readily available funds will be. This amount will then be kept aside for this purpose. The amount is based on feeling rather than fact.

Keeping Cash on Hand

The cost of keeping cash at hand should be compared with the benefits derived from it. The cost of keeping cash can be equated with the expected return when it is held in some alternative investment. This implies that you should not keep excessive amounts of cash as there will be a loss of income. This reduced income should be balanced with the risk of not having it when needed.

The optimum amount of readily available money to keep is normally calculated by large companies who utilize complex cash management models. It would be wise for the normal sized household to consider the factors mentioned above when considering the amount of money to keep available for each of the reasons mentioned above.

The amount could be adjusted over time, based on your experience. In the final analysis, it should be remembered that CASH is KING and if you have it you can dictate the terms and conditions of most purchases.

It is always beneficial to build up a good relationship with your banker. They are mostly in a better position to guide in respect of the total cost of financing and cash flow benefits. Even it todays world of online banking the bank manager or personal banker, is a valuable asset.

Understanding Profit and Loss

The adage that, what you can measure is what you can manage, is just as true for your finances as for any other activity. In order to measure your profit, you need to follow a certain set of rules in order to be able to compare your results with others.

Profit is your incentive for being in business; without profit, you will lose interest and after a while will not bother. Profit is your reward for taking the risk to be in business. One should understand that generally speaking the higher the risk the higher the reward (or loss if it goes wrong) and the lower the low risk the lower the reward.

It is true that nobody will take any risks without a suitable reward in return for taking the risk. All business is risky (some more than others) so no reward (profits) means no business. This article addresses profits and loss and provides some insight into the account drawn up to record the information.

The purpose of this article is to provide a basic understanding of the components of a profit and loss statement that a startup entrepreneur should use to enable him or her to become financially independent.

The Profit and Loss Statement

When one looks at a profit and loss statement drafted by an accountant it looks like a very complex document. Whatever format the profit and loss statement is in, the basis of the document is to systematically summarize the revenues, costs and expenses incurred during a specific period of time.

The profit and loss account is significantly different from the balance sheet as it is a record of the business trading activities over a given period of time or for a specific project. On the other hand, the balance sheet is a snapshot of financial position of the business at a point in time.

The Profit and Loss Statement Frequency

The norm is to get a statement like this produced by the auditor or accountant at least once a year.

Any acute businessperson will tell you that one cannot manage a company on information received once a year only, and therefore it is strongly recommended that the timing of the profit and loss statement should be aligned with the frequency of the activity that is measured. It may be necessary to draw up a profit and loss statement at the conclusion of each significant event or milestone in a project. In some cases, it is necessary to have the profit and loss statement up to date and live all the time to ensure the profitability of a project.

It is always better to make use of an automated system to generate your profits and losses. This can be in the form of a simple excel spreadsheet. If you do not have the skills to make one yourself you can always get a good one online for a few dollars. This is an easy accounting system, designed in Excel, which is intended to help you manage your domestic and business accounts. What I like most about this software is that it looks just like a bank statement and one does not need to have special skills to run it. Its limitation is that once your company grows you will need more advanced software, but for the price, it is really worthwhile getting this.

The reason why this is so important is that these records provide information that shows the ability of an entity to generate profit by increasing revenue and reducing costs. In certain circles, the profit and loss statement is also known as an income statement or an income and expense statement.

The Profit and Loss Statement Structure

The profit and loss statement generally follows a standard format however the format is less important than the accuracy of the information.

The statement begins with an item for revenue or sales. This is followed by the costs of operating the business. This is normally subdivided into a section called the cost of sales and the operating expenses.

The cost of sales is nothing else than the cost of preparing the goods sold in a format where it is ready to deliver to a customer. This normally includes all production and raw material cost.

The operating expenses comprise of items like marketing and sales costs, research and developing cost and general administrative and overheads costs.

The final section contains the tax and interest and finally, the distributable profit or loss is revealed.

Calculating Profit and Loss

Starting with the revenue or sales one deducts the costs of sales for this. The revenue is the money you receive from the sales made. It can be complicated but a simple example will suffice.

If you have sold 100 items for $1-00 each and gave customers discount on items sold to the value of $5-00 your sales income will be $95-00

The cost of sales includes all the cost directly associated with preparing the item ready for sale. Remember to include labour and raw material cost that can be directly linked to the production unit. If the labour cost came to $20-00 to produce the 100 items and the total raw material cost per product was $0-25 per item the cost of sales would be $45-00 [$20-00 %2B (100 X $0.25) = $45-00]

This calculation results in the figure known as the gross profit. In our example the gross profit will therefore be $50-00 [$95-00 - $45-00 = $50-00].

The operating expenses are calculated next. This normally constitutes of marketing and sales costs, research and developing cost and general administrative and overheads costs. The operating expenses are normally not traceable to a single produced or sold the product. Once the operating expenses are deducted from the gross profit you will have your operating profit or also sometimes called EBIT (Earnings Before Interest and Tax). If you calculate the operating expenses at $ 20-00 for the particular project the operating profit will come to $30-00 [$50-00 - $20-00 = $30-00].

In order to calculate your net profit, you need to deduct all taxes and interest expense. For the purposes of this example, no tax and interest are accounted for. In some cases, the profit and loss statement continues to reflect how much money is distributed to shareholders and how much is kept behind to finance future projects. It is also this figure that the accountant would normally transfer to your balance sheet.

There is a number of websites from where you can download free profit and loss statements templates (normally an excel spreadsheet template). The best idea is to download one of these and then customize it for your own situation.

Uses of the Profit and Loss Account

The primary use of the profit and loss statement is to monitor and measure profit, as discussed above. For this reason, one needs to ensure that the information recording is accurate. To this end, you need to make sure that you include all relevant costs. Significant problems can arise if the information is inaccurate. You may be under the impression that your company is making a profit and growing but in reality, you are slowly going out of business.

Once you have accurately calculated the profit or in some cases the loss, the information can be used for judging how well the business is doing compared to itself in the past, compared to the managers' plans and compared to other businesses. It will also assist you to adjust your cost structure as you will be able to see profit leaks that you may not have been aware previously.

Why is the Paperwork Necessary

It is always a struggle to get entrepreneurs to do administration as most of them fly by the seat of their pants. If you wish to be successful and is not one of those few geniuses that can see the profit or loss without doing any calculations, you have to force yourself to record at least the income and expense information and use it as explained above.

Knowing which projects are making a profit and which are losing income and then taking the necessary action to rectify it is an integral part of becoming financially independent.

I Got Too Much Debt, What Now?

Getting Out of Your Debt Spiral

If you feel like a small ship with a broken rudder on a large and stormy ocean when you look at your debt you are probably hoping for some sort of miracle to happen. A lot of op people in this situation revert to gambling solutions such as plying the Lotto. Well, unfortunately for those who employ this type of tactics there is only bad news, as this will only result in heartache and financial disaster. Statistically speaking you have an extremely small chance of winning the jackpot. This type of spending should be avoided completely. In any event, it is much better to invest your available cash in something that you may have some control over.

The miracle you need may rather be found in one of these ways discussed in this article to lower your debt payments. There are no guarantees in life and following the advice in this article may also not produce the desired outcome, but at least following these recommendations will give you the best chance you have to come out in some reasonable form on the other side.

If your financial position is such that it feels to you that it is getting out of control, the time has come that you take real quick action in order to resolve the situation.

The Road to Recovery

To get out of debt, you need to follow a structured approach. It is probably at least partially a lack of structure and planning that go you into the debt position you are in. In order to ensure that the road to recovery results in a solution that is sustainable, you need to follow a structured approach.

Evaluate the Historic Path to Your Current Financial Position

You may want to bury the painful past as soon as possible, however irrespective of how painful it is you need to evaluate all the activities that contributed to your current financial position. It is very rare that your debt will be out of control as a result of one or two events. It is more likely that the debt position came about as a result of a sequence of events that was long in the making.

The biggest mistake you can make is to focus on the last straw that broke the camel's back. If your inability to service your debt is as a result of you lost your job take care not to only focus on this event. Also look at the timing and type of debt you ran up. Valuable lessons can be learnt from carefully considering these and other factors.

Objectively Assess Your Financial Situation

You may like you are having a bad dream and the faster you try to run the more you are tangling in the unseen tentacles and the monster is getting closer and closer. Like in a bad dream the best tactics are to wake up. In financial terms that imply that you must objectively assess your financial position. If you look at all your debt and all your available cash as well as the sources of funds available you may see that the debt monster is only a bad dream. If after doing this you still do not see the light the next step is to negotiate with creditors.

Negotiate With Creditors

The people who offered you the debt in the first instance are normally in the best position to assist. It also makes sense to talk to them as they have an interest in resolving the issue amicably.

The first step is to make a list of your current debtors. Make sure that you do not leave anybody out. The obvious ones are those ones that send you monthly statements, but also consider the debts that have different payment intervals like the quarterly payments required by some institutions as well as an annual payment that may be required. The fact that some of these payments may only be required to be made some time in the future is irrelevant as it is payments that you must plan for.

Once you have come up with the list of people and institutions that you owe money to note the total amount owed to each. The interval payments (such as instalments) must also be recorded against each creditor's name. With this information, you should calculate how much you can afford to pay each creditor. Be fair and equitable when doing this calculation and keep a careful record of the criteria used, you may have to explain your thinking later.

Armed with this information, make an appointment to see the person in charge of each of your accounts. Be well prepared when you go to the meetings and explain that you are willing to pay the debt but can only afford to pay the amount you calculated. If the person is not prepared to or in a position to agree to the reduced payment amount make an appointment with a more senior person and keep a record of who you contacted as well as the outcome of each meeting. Never say that you cannot afford to pay the debt as this can be seen as a declaration of insolvency and may be used against you later.

Once you get to an agreement make sure that you get the agreement in writing, preferably on a company letterhead. Ensure that you then make the payments in accordance with this agreement.

Avoid New Debts

In order to get out of debt, it goes without saying that more debt is an absolute no-no. You have to be careful in times like this as it may seem like a good idea to take more debt. The problem is that you are just postponing the inevitable as all debt have to be settled at some time and if you cannot afford to service existing debt your position will just be worse when the time comes that you have to start paying the new debt.

You should avoid using credit cards, even if they offer free credit for a period of time. In fact, a good strategy would be to cancel all the credit cards you have a zero balance. Also make sure you cancel all agreements that require regular payments, especially those that add little value to your lifestyle or that you seldom use but still pay for.

You should endeavour to stop utilizing credit for your daily living expenses altogether.

Control Spending

Everybody agrees that you must continue living and that costs money. The problem is that it may be your lifestyle that contributed to the current financial position. You should evaluate all expenses you make. A good idea is to have a philosophy that you will not spend money on what you need but rather limit expenses to items you cannot go without. To have control over your spending you need to have a clear understanding of all your monthly income and expenses and try to find out if you're spending more than you are earning.

Remember that you MUST prevent excessive expenses if you want any chance of a sustainable debt clearance solution. In order to provide you with assistance with this, you must develop a comprehensive expense budget and stick to it.

Increase Income

It is only logical that your debt position must improve if you increase your income. Most authors on this subject recommend this but few give practical solutions in this regard. In order to increase the income, you first have to understand the basics. A day is conveniently divided into three eight hour shifts. Most people work the first shift to make ends meet and rest or sleep the second shit to be fresh to work the first shift. The key to success lies in the third shift. Successful people all have one thing in common they utilize the third shift successfully.

There are a number of things you can do during this shift to get out of debt and even get to a financial position where you could be financially independent. Remember that your capital investment is available for all three shifts, you may want to consider utilizing this investment better. By just spending on the variable cost component your net profit may increaser, making it possible to reduce your debt. There are a number of other ways that you can utilize to generate some extra cash, do not be afraid to ask your auditor or other advisor about this.

Final Words

If you want to get out of a debt spiral you have to know choice but to develop a structured approach to resolve issues with your creditors and also manage your finances better. In addition, it is a good idea to improve your position by utilizing the so-called third shift.

Using Financial Statements for Decision-making

The Financial statements of a company or individual are the documents that reflect the historical financial information of the entity. This includes a detailed and accurate record of the assets and liabilities as well as the income and expenses and also the cash flow of the entity.

The Financial Statements

Financial statement as communications medium provides a valuable summary of the entities economic history. It is useful to establish the performance as well as the future potential of the entity. The basic definitions of the main components of the financial statements are:

The Balance sheet - this is a record of the assets and liabilities on a given date.

The Income statement - this is a record of the income and expenses for the reporting period.

The Cash Flow statement - this is a record of the sources and application of funds that includes operating, investment, and financing activities and how they impacted on the cash position during the reporting period.

The Purpose of Financial Statements

The primary purpose of the accountant is to provide appropriate information in a standardized format for the taking of financially based decisions. For this purpose, the financial statements generally follow a standardized structure. The financial statements are a record of the activities but do not provide an evaluation of the data. Despite the important role of the financial statements they do not provide an evaluation of the accounting results. In order to be able to use the information contained in the various financial statements for financial decision-making, a number of measurements and evaluations needs to be made to the numbers. Only then will the information be useful as a tool for decision-making.

The Purpose of Measurement and Evaluation

The purpose of the conducting measurements and making an evaluation is to provide answers to the following questions:

- Why there are no excess funds available?
- Are the reporting entity financially sound?
- Would it be possible to make further loans?
- Will available cash generating be sufficient to provide in the anticipated demand?

The format and type of information obtained during this process will depend on the intended users of the information.

Interpreting the Numbers

The conducting measurements and the making of evaluation process basically consist of the rearranging of the information in order to obtain information in a format that can be used to appraise the performance, activities, financial health, stability and growth potential.

In order to conduct a proper evaluation and interpretation of financial statements, the following important steps need to be followed.

Conduct a superficial analysis of the financial statements in order to obtain an initial feeling for the areas that need special attention. Conduct an evaluation of the flow of funds in order to establish the ability of the entity to generate cash as well as the needs for funds. Conduct a ratio analysis in relation to rentability also sometimes called profitability, Risk and Growth Analysis of non-financial information

From the above introduction to financial statements, it is clear that not all the information necessary to make sound financial decisions is readily available form these statements. A number of ratios need to be calculated and compared with others to enable the decision maker to draw the correct conclusions. It should be remembered that the financial statements reflect the historic activities and that decisions are taken about the future. This can only be done by drawing conclusions about trends of the different ratios rather than the actual historic numbers.

The Time Value of Money

Understanding the time value of money will assist you to make better investment decisions. The basic idea behind the time value of money is that money has different values depending on when it is received. The risk assassinated with whether or not money will be received in the future will influence the value of the proceeds.

The concepts associated with the time value of money has a lot of practical applications and can be of significant value in determining the best investment to make.

Would you rather have $ 1,000-00 today or $ 1,000 in 5 years? If you are like most people the obvious answer is to want the $ 1,000-00 today. The truth is five years is a long time to wait. During the five years, a lot of things can go wrong and you may never see the $ 1,000-00. Why would any reasonable individual postpone receiving money to the future when he or she could have the same amount of money now? For the majority of people, having the money now is just common sense.

This is understandable as any money you receive today can be used to fund investment or for consumption purposes immediately. This implies that the sooner one receives money the sooner it can be put to work. This concept is referred to as the Time Value of Money!

The question clearly is why to focus on the time when money is involved. Well, time affords one the opportunity to immediately start earning interest on the money. Not having the opportunity to earn interest on money is generally called the opportunity cost.

Comparing Amounts at Different Times

The question that inevitably comes to mind is how one can compare amounts at different time periods. It should be clear that one cannot compare the value of money that is available at different times without adjusting the values for the various durations.

The primary factor that influences the value of the adjustment is the risk associated with waiting for the money. This risk is expressed as an interest rate.

To determine the value of money at different times one can use an interest rate that reflects the risk associated with the situation and time. The interest rate is often defined by the price of money. It may be useful to remember that the interest rate is normally expressed as a percentage of the principal value.

Simplifying the concept, the amount charged by a lender to a borrower for the use of assets, typically for a period of one year, divided by the principle value of the assets expressed as a percentage is known as the annual rate percentage.

In other words, the interest rate is the rate which is charged, paid or sacrificed for the use of money or asset for the given time period. In the next section, the various concepts will be explained further.

Present Value

In order to further clarify the concept, one needs to understand a few critical terms. The first of these is "Present Value". If one receives the $ 1,000-00 today, the present value would, of course, be $ 1,000-00, because the value of the amount at present is what you receive today.

Interest rates often change as a result of inflation and other associated risks. For example, if a lender charges a lender $ 90-00 in a year on a loan of $ 1000-00, then the interest rate would be [(90÷1000)X(100÷1)] = 9%.

In other words If $ 1000-00 is deposited in a savings account that pays 9% interest annually, with interest paid at the end of the year, then at the end of the year, $ 90-00 of interest will be added to the $ 1000-00 principal amount resulting in a total of $1090-00 in your hand.

This can be expressed by an equation as follows. If the principal amount is represented as a P and the interest rate per year is expressed as i, then the amount of money available at the end of the year can be expressed by the equation P x (1 + i).

Future Value

If the $ 1,000-00 were only received in one year's time, the present value of the amount would not be $ 1,000-00 because you do not have it in your hand today. That implies that some amounts will be expressed as a "Future Value". The future value can be defined as the total value of an amount you will receive at the end of the period. In order to determine the present value of the $ 1,000-00 you will receive at the end of the year, you need to treat the $ 1,000-00 as the future value. To compare the $ 1000-00 received today with the same amount received in one year one needs to find the present value of the future $ 1,000-00. Another way to look at it is to calculate how much you would have to invest today in order to receive the $ 1,000-00 in one year from today. This process is called discounting.

Discounting

Discounting is the process of determining the present value of future value. This is the reverse of determining the future value of a payment, as in this instance the future value is already known. The present value is calculated by dividing the future value by the interest factor. The interest factor is reflected by the expression $(1 + i) n$, where i is the annual interest rate expressed as a decimal and n is the number of years.

There are three factors that govern the present value of a future value. The first one is the size of the future value. Is should be obvious that the larger the future value, the larger the present value.

The second one is the risk associated with receiving the future value. As the uncertainty of receiving the future value increases, the expectation to receive a future certain value decreases which decrease the value that should be paid today for that future value. The risk is expressed as the interest rate.

The third factor is the time period that will have to be waited to receive the future value. The longer one has to wait, the less value the future value will have. The duration reduces the present value of a future value more and more as the time increases as uncertainty increases into the future.

Market and Sell

Many small business owners can confirm that when you run your own business, every dollar you save can make a big difference. Unfortunately, there are some costs to doing business that you just can't avoid. However, there can also be many simple and easy ways to help save money.

Without sales, you have no business. The proof of concept for your business idea is that a sufficient number of people are prepared to pay you more for the product or service you build your business on than the costs to you to provide it.

In order to make sales, your potential customers must know about your product. Without going into the nuances and theory of marketing, the process of informing potential customers about your product is called marketing. Selling, in essence, is getting them to part with their money in exchange for your product or service. You may offer a product that is in high demand for a fraction of the going price, but unless potential customers know about it, they will not buy from you.

Marketing

Marketing is very diverse and can have many components, ingredients and elements. It is clear to the serious student that marketing does not have a constant definition. It is a concept that evolves with the situation and the environment.

To different people, it means different things. To some, it will be a philosophy of business. To others, it will be a management function or a management process. Another group sees marketing as a social process or a social science.

According to the American Marketing Association, the definition of marketing can be summarized as follows:

> *"Marketing is the process and execution of the conception, pricing, promotion, and distribution of ideas, goods and services to create exchanges that satisfy individual and organizational goals"*

Since around 1970 this definition has been in general use in countless textbooks and training manuals. It reflects different important concepts of marketing. This definition includes the double dimension of strategic and operational marketing, the 4P's of marketing, the different application of marketing that includes ideas, concepts physical goods as well as service and also reflects the marketing objective of mutual satisfaction between the customer and the marketer.

In order to effectively integrate marketing functions, three interdependent primary marketing functions must be conducted by you the entrepreneur, as follows:

Marketing Research

Companies need very specific marketing information in order to introduce products or services that will create value for both the customers and the companies. One needs to clearly distinguish between market research that is specifically focused on the markets, while marketing research is paying exclusive attention to the processes involved in marketing. One would engage in marketing research to identify and solve marketing problems that may be encountered.

Marketing research includes conducting marketing studies in the form of surveys or focuses group discussions for example. These methods can be either qualitative or quantitative in nature, depending on the situation and the specific need.

When conducting marketing research it is often the case that more than one research method and style is used to ensure a balanced view of the research results.

The purpose of this types of marketing research is often to establish the positioning of the competitors and to scientifically develop plans to control the effectiveness of the marketing effort.

Strategic Marketing

The main aim of the strategic marketing function is to focus the often limited resources of an organization on the most suitable prospective marketing segments with the aim of increasing sales and reaching a position where a sustainable competitive advantage can be maintained.

The starting point is normally to choose a suitable target market for the product or range of products of the company. The strategic marketing function also includes defining the product concept or services as this will directly influence the strategic position of the company in the marketplace. In order to do this, the marketing team needs to define the desired positioning of the company or the brand positioning of the specific products or services.

The pricing strategy will be informed by the strategic position of the company and can be different in different marketing segments.

The strategic function is responsible for choosing suitable distribution channels and determining the relationship with distributors in respect of the product or service.

The key components of the communication strategy will flow from the marketing strategy and should be utilized by the operational marketing team as a basis for marketing communications.

The relationship strategy should be determined as part of the marketing strategy to ensure that the strategic positioning is maintained during operational marketing activities.

Operational Marketing

Every element of the operational marketing initiatives should be based on the formal strategic marketing plan.

The operational marketing function normally includes the building of the promotion and operational communications campaign. It also includes close interaction with the sales team. Distribution and merchandising normally forms an integral part of the operational marketing function when the product line consists of fast moving consumer goods.

Other types of functions include some direct marketing activities and a strong focus on customer service.

Selecting the Optimum Marketing Mix

The marketing mix model discussed in this section is known as the 4 P's marketing mix model and can be used by companies as a tool to achieve its marketing objectives.

The purpose of using a marketing mix model such as the 4P's model is to help develop an optimum combination of decisions in an objective manner that will satisfy the needs of the customers and potential customers in the selected target market as well as to maximize the ability of the company to achieve its overall goals and objectives.

The correct use of the 4P's will help companies to effectively define the marketing elements necessary for successfully positioning of the product range in the identified target market.

Using and Understanding the 4 P's Marketing Mix Model

No company or individual can continue to be in business successfully without selling either a product or a service. In order to sell successfully, an effective marketing strategy should be implemented. The correct marketing strategy is the one that has the biggest potential to ensure a sustainable sales volume growth for the particular business. The challenge is to correctly evaluate the available options and implement the strategy that is most suited for the situation. The business strategy should be aligned with the marketing strategy as a minimum.

When evaluating the marketing strategy one should have a clear understanding of how to leverage the product, price, promotion, and place related to the marketing objectives of the company. These four parameters are often referred to as the 4 P's of the marketing mix and represent the different choices a company can make in the complex process of successfully bringing a product or service to market.

Marketing decisions generally fall into one of these four controllable parameters in an attempt to generate a buy response from potential clients in the target market.

The individual marketing decision about the marketing mix criteria will be discussed individually in this article however it is important to remember that they should be evaluated for their cross-impact regarding the way in which they are affecting the other three parameters.

Product Decisions

In marketing terms, the expression product refers to any product or service. Product decisions are often misunderstood to only be the type of product or service. Product decisions also include decisions about the product brand, name and position as well as the functionality, styling, quality, safety and packaging of the product or service. All these items will influence the perception that potential clients will have about the product and therefore great care should be taken with these aspects.

Price Decisions

One of the more commonly known P of the four P's is the price parameter. Price decisions are primarily about setting the correct base price but also include decisions about the positioning of the product or service. This includes issues about the marketing objectives like to ensure survival, maximize profit, ensure market share leadership or establish product quality leadership. The strategy can be to penetrate or hold a market position. Price decisions also include determining the suggested retail price and whether or not volume or another discount will be applicable. In some cases, the seasonality of the product may also require that a different price should be effective at different times.

Promotion Decisions

The most well-known marketing parameter is this factor. Promotion refers to the different aspects of the marketing communication strategy. Marketing communication is primarily conducted with the task of conveying information about the product to customers and potential customers with the aim of influencing their purchasing decisions in a positive manner.

The four primary areas that should be considered is; advertising, sales promotions, personal selling and public relations. These decisions will then be translated into a promotional strategy and will result in marketing communications budget.

Place Decisions

The place decisions are about the distribution required to get the product available, at the right time, at the right place, in the right quantities. These decisions include obvious items about the logistics to get the product or service to the customer that includes warehousing, distribution centres, transportation and reverse logistics. It also includes decisions about less obvious issues such as the selection of distribution channels for the product or product range, the extent of the market coverage and inventory management.

Marketing Tools

In real life, marketing often revolves around the implementation and execution of a number of practical, logical and sensible actions that will address the defined marketing factors. One should remember that life is not a set of textbook perfect situations and marketing information can change in a very short time span. Normally real companies have limited resources that are further complicated by the uncertainties of market segments that are not perfectly homogeneous and timescales that are normally tough to deal with.

Under these real-life situations, the classical marketing techniques are often only implemented in an irregular and partial manner. The marketer who can make the necessary adjustments "on the fly" will be viewed as the marketing wizard, while the slow mover will be lost in the annals of marketing case studies when students are taught how not to react to market needs.

Marketing can be a very expensive activity. There is a lot that start-up business can do to cut this cost item down to affordable levels. Being a small business gives the entrepreneur the ideal opportunity to support a startup marketing company that has a lower cost structure than the majors.

In addition to this, there is a lot than the entrepreneur can do him or herself in respect of marketing material.

Some of the so-called traditional marketing materials you can start creating without any real problem includes:

Brochures

A marketing brochure is a printed piece of information, often in the form of a booklet. A Brochure is one of a number of printed possibilities that a business can utilize for product promotion and marketing. This is a particularly useful and important instrument used for marketing by small businesses. One of the primary benefits of using brochures is the versatility of this marketing device. As a result of the booklet format, offer much more space for information than other printed marketing materials.

The entrepreneur can create professional looking brochures on a laptop with standard available software. With the advent of social media, it is important to design these in such a manner that it can be used electronically as well.

Mailers

Do not underestimate the power of snail mail as a marketing tool. Snail mail has recently been used as the most novel and effective marketing delivery mechanism. The rewards of direct mail campaigns can exceed every other marketing campaign if done correctly. Mailers got a bad name before mail merge and high-quality in-house printing was generally available. One of the keys to a successful mailer campaign is to make every individual item look like quality, are personalized having the correct name and address on the envelope and the mailer and have a personal touch like a being signed with a pen and not a computer.

A well-designed, personalized, printed sales or service letter can be professionally done in minutes using standard word processing tools that come on every office computer. These can then be mailed to individuals at a fraction of the cost of newspaper ads for example. It may be a good idea to place stamps on the letters rather than bulk post them as it may just get the letter to the intended person.

Posters

A marketing poster allows you to communicate and reach a large audience in a specific geographical area at a reasonable cost, and in a very short period. A well-designed poster can function as a semi-permanent attention-grabbing marketing tool.

Political parties know the value of a well-placed poster. Many startup businesses do not make use of this relatively cheap and effective marketing method. By designing and printing posters locally, you can promote your products, services or events quickly, easily and professionally to your geographical market.

When you want to make use of this form of marketing, ensure that you know the local law and regulations about displaying posters. You will almost certainly be prohibited from interfering with traffic signs and some of the local bylaws may prohibit you from displaying any poster unless the local council has approved it. You may also need to make a deposit that you can forfeit if you do not remove the posters before a certain date.

Business Cards

An often-overlooked marketing tool is the business card. This cheap and powerful marketing tool can be created and printed by the entrepreneur. Remember that a business card has two sides and the back should be used as marketing space.

Loyalty Cards

Most startup business owners overlook this or think that it is primarily for large businesses like airlines. In reality, studies proved that the smallest coffee shop can double its sales by the introduction of a simple low cost printed loyalty card and managing these correctly

Part of your marketing is to have a feedback mechanism in place where your customers can give you feedback. Setting up such a feedback channel should not be done only because "it is the correct thing to do" in fact, you should actually listen to your customers. Their feedback and input are among the most critical information you will ever learn, therefore it is imperative that you act upon it. It is a well-known fact that repeat business is the easiest business to get.

Electronic Marketing

Electronic marketing keeps on growing as a percentage of total market spent, this despite the fact that cost for Electronic marketing keeps on shrinking. There could be many reasons for this, which falls outside the scope of this publication. The important part is to ensure that your startup business has a presence in the electronic media.

The absolute minimum requirement is that you have a company e-Mail address that you do not use for any personal communication. Set it up in such a manner that you have a default signature that not only tell people who you are but what the business can help them with. In other words put some marketing thought into what your business signature will consist of.

Depending on the type of industry you are in, your next most important electronic asset as far as marketing is concerned is a Company Website that reflects the culture and values of your business. There are many options available (some free or very cheap) that you can use here.

The trouble of where to go next starts at this point. Some proponents swear by the Company Facebook route (sometimes even before the Company Website). Others think that Twitter or Instagram will be better and yet another group believe in having a presence on LinkedIn, Snapchat or eBay. You can believe me if I say, if you as 10 people which one is a must you will get 12 opinions. I personally think that you need to analyze your business needs, look at the profile of your ideal customer and compare that with what every one of these options (and they are growing fast) offer. Select the one or two that aligns best with your business needs and customer profile and make them work effectively before you move on to others.

As electronic marketing very specialized, I strongly recommend you first read a good publication on this topic and then interview a number of different service providers that will suit your needs.

With the meteoric rise of e-businesses and electronic technology, most people think that this is the way to go with marketing. It would be completely wrong to ignore the internet and many social media platforms out there

Sales

To make a sale a customer must interact with the business or its agents. This can be in person, via an agent, a telephone or the internet.

As the sales process is the lifeblood of your business the sales channels that you select for your business is of extreme importance. Some businesses will have to make use of more than one sales channel.

The coffee shop example mentioned above understood this and invested in a website where registered loyalty cardholders could order a drink to be ready at a given time (with a repeat option). This reduced the waiting time for customers on the go and increased the sales even further.

Being creative with the sales channels are your only limiting factor, but remember that the sale is not complete until the invoice is paid.

Another important part of securing sales is determining the correct price. You may think that the lower the price the better the sales. A number of practical studies proved that if the price is too low the sales reduce. Most people will gladly pay a price if they feel that it is the correct price to pay for the article, even if your margin for the product is a 1000%. Getting sales at best price is always a losing strategy for a startup, as your established competitors will be able to outlast you in any price war.

Run a Professional Business

Far too many entrepreneurs run their business like an extension of their personal lives. This is the worst mistake an entrepreneur can make. It is important to set up a suitable legal business entity and keep it separate from your personal life. You may enjoy the initial freedom that an integrated business and personal life can give you but will regret this integration soon.

By separating your personal life from the business, you will have the benefit of being a professional businessperson irrespective of the size of the business. This will ensure that, when conducting business, any personal issue does not hold you back. This separation includes family and friends enjoying benefits from the business without formally contributing to its success. Employing family or friends may seem a good idea and often works well, but not everybody has the ability to separate work from private life. Should a situation occur that, a family member or friend, needs to be disciplined for a business related issue, you may find that the nepotism is more costly than the few dollars you may have saved by employing them.

Like in most companies, you will have some

form of intellectual property that makes your business unique. It is your fiduciary duty as an entrepreneur to protect and defend your company's intellectual property.

In order to do this, you need to know the difference between a copyright, trademark, trade secrets, and patent. If you do not protect and defend your intellectual property, you will lose your only competitive advantage.

One's private life can be based on informal verbal agreements. However, a business runs on written and formal agreements. You need to learn to read and write effective agreements. Agreements are the basis of your business processes. These can include formal agreements or contracts with suppliers, employees or clients. The main point here is to ensure that all and any agreement is in writing and that you understand your responsibilities and benefits as contained in the agreement. You know the expression "good fences make good neighbours?" It is the same in business. The more effective your agreements are, the better your business relationships will be.

A wise man once told me that running away could be a good thing, as long as you start running in time. As a successful business owner, you also need to know when to call it quits. Do not let your ego take you on a journey you cannot complete. It is important to know when to hold and when to fold. If your idea does not work out the way you planned, be big enough to accept it and shut it down. Assess what you would have done differently. Determine how you will utilize these hard-learned lessons to improve your next venture and move on. Failure is inevitable, but a true entrepreneur will prevail over adversity.

No business book or business plan can predict the future or fully prepare you to become a successful entrepreneur. There is no such thing as the perfect plan. There is no perfect road or one less travelled. Never jump right into a new business without any thought or planning, but do not spend months or years waiting to execute. You will become a well-rounded entrepreneur when tested under fire. The most important thing you can do is learn from your mistakes--and never make the same mistake twice. All you are achieving by not learning from your mistakes are that you will throw your hard-earned money into a hole in the ground.

Page intentionally left blank

Conclusion

Every failed business have a very specific reason for failing. It is a fact that most business failures can be traced back to business leaders who did not see the problems in time or saw it but elected to ignore it. As an entrepreneur, you will be faced with a multitude of business-related information. It is your main duty as a business leader to interpret the signs and signals and act on it. In cases that you are uncertain as to the potential impact or consequences of signals, you should be strong enough to ask professionals for guidance in the interest of your business' survival. Do not become a legend in your own mind because you were too proud to ask for assistance to save your business. Before it is too late, ask for help and become a real legend

---oOo---

References

The content of this e-book is broadly based on my personal business experience and studies that I have done over the years and I refer to is as common sense.

In the knowledge explosion times, we live in, most of the information contained in the e-book is probably available in some form or another, from a variety of sources. In order for me to give the original author of these ideas suitable recognition would be very difficult and in many cases impossible to achieve.

If anybody feels the need to be individually recognized, please feel free to send me your dated publication and I will include you as a reference if warranted.

www.ingramcontent.com/pod-product-compliance
Lightning Source LLC
Chambersburg PA
CBHW031448210526
45464CB00005B/2373